Where do you want to go?

To gal the m for the co signs or ask a guide!

You choose...

Nature's Cathedral

Step inside one of London's most amazing buildings.

What makes the Museum look like a cathedral?

The Natural History Museum was built in the 1870s. The building is decorated with tiles and features made of baked clay, called terracotta. What other features make it look like a cathedral?

Big bird

Moas were giant birds that lived in New Zealand. How much taller is our moa than you? Moas were wiped out about 600 years ago, after people first arrived in New Zealand.

Explore the displays around the Central Hall which show off some of the Museum's special specimens.

I spy *terracotta*

How many of these clay creatures can you spot inside and outside the Museum?

**Bat   Kangaroo   Lion   Monkey
Octopus   Owl   Pterosaur**

Ice Age animal

The giant armadillo lived in South America during the Ice Ages. It could draw its head inside the bony covering to protect itself. The giant armadillo died out 10,000 years ago.

Fatal accident

This huge amphibian may have been killed by a falling tree about 235 million years ago. The body became covered in mud at the bottom of a lake. The mud eventually turned to rock while the bones disintegrated. The cavity left behind was filled with plaster to make this cast.

Extinct amphibian

The biggest living thing

At the top of the *Central Hall's* staircase is a slice of a giant sequoia's trunk. The giant sequoia from California, USA is the world's largest living thing because of its bulk. One of its relatives, the coast redwood, is the tallest tree.

How old? The tree was a seedling in AD 557. How old was the tree when it was cut down in 1892?

Find out about amphibians on page 14

Painted plants

Look up at the ceiling in the *Central Hall*. Can you see the panels showing different kinds of plants? This one shows the seed pods of the cacao plant from which chocolate is made.

Dinosaurs

Come face to face with some of the scariest animals that ever lived on land.

What is a dinosaur?

Dinosaurs walked with their legs held straight underneath their body. This helped them to walk or run better than other reptiles like lizards. Most dinosaurs had scaly skins but some had feathers like birds.

Monitor lizard

Triceratops (Try-ser-ah-tops) dinosaur

Splayed legs

Straight legs

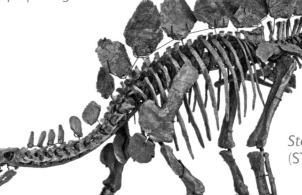

Stegosaurus (STEG-oh-SORE-us)

Great shape

Dinosaurs had shapes that seem strange to us today. This North American dinosaur had 19 plates along its back that would have made it a bony mouthful.

Two feet or four feet

The biggest dinosaurs plodded along on four feet. They had pillar-like legs to support their bulky bodies. The fastest dinosaurs ran along on two legs. *Gallimimus* was a fast runner that used speed to escape danger. *Iguanodon* could walk on four feet and may have also stood up on its back legs like a bear.

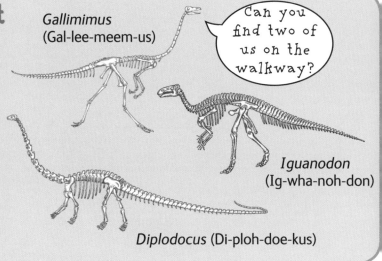

Gallimimus (Gal-lee-meem-us)

Can you find two of us on the walkway?

Iguanodon (Ig-wha-noh-don)

Diplodocus (Di-ploh-doe-kus)

How many kinds of dinosaur?

Scientists have discovered about 600 different kinds of dinosaur. Over half of these are known only from a few of their fossil bones. Scientists still discover new kinds of dinosaur today by digging up new fossils and by studying fossil specimens in museum collections.

New find

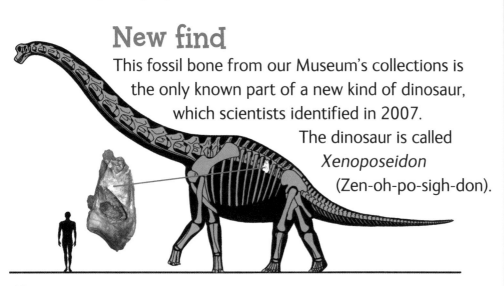

This fossil bone from our Museum's collections is the only known part of a new kind of dinosaur, which scientists identified in 2007. The dinosaur is called *Xenoposeidon* (Zen-oh-po-sigh-don).

Super-size me

Some of the dinosaurs were the largest animals that ever lived on land. Some kinds reached taller than the treetops and weighed at least twelve times more than an elephant. These gigantic dinosaurs ate plants. Our biggest dinosaur is the *Diplodocus* (Di-ploh-doe-kus) skeleton in the *Central Hall*.

Small ones

Dromaeosaurus (Dro-may-oh-sore-us) was about the height of a large dog. They hunted in packs to bring down prey larger than themselves. The smallest dinosaurs were about the size of a chicken and ate small prey, such as insects.

Dinosaurs

Discover what scientists learn about the lives of dinosaurs by studying their fossils.

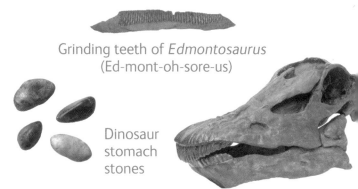

Did you know dinosaur footprints are a kind of fossil?

Match the heads

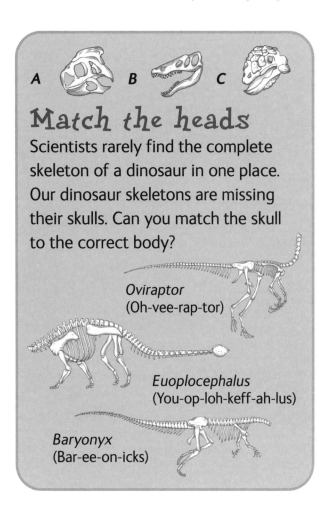

A **B** **C**

Scientists rarely find the complete skeleton of a dinosaur in one place. Our dinosaur skeletons are missing their skulls. Can you match the skull to the correct body?

Oviraptor
(Oh-vee-rap-tor)

Euoplocephalus
(You-op-loh-keff-ah-lus)

Baryonyx
(Bar-ee-on-icks)

Grinding teeth of *Edmontosaurus*
(Ed-mont-oh-sore-us)

Dinosaur stomach stones

Raking front teeth of *Diplodocus*

Veggies

Some dinosaurs only ate plants. The large, long-necked dinosaurs had raking teeth to tear off leaves from the treetops. To grind the leaves up, they swallowed stones that churned around in their stomachs. Other plant-eating dinosaurs had multiple rows of grinding teeth.

Bony heads

Male *Pachycephalosaurus* (Pack-ee-keff-ah-low-sore-us) were thought to head-butt each other in competition over females. Their thick bony skulls probably protected their rather small brains.

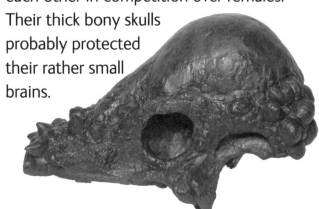

Noisy neighbours

Parasaurolophus, (Par-ah-sore-ol-oh-fus) could warn others in its herd of danger by blowing air through the crest on its head. This made a low trumpeting sound.

Meet me for lunch

Do you think *Tyrannosaurus* (Tie-ran-oh-sore-us) was a blood-thirsty hunter or do you think it scavenged from carcasses of dead animals? The chances are it may have done both. What we know for certain is that its jaws were strong and armed with sharp curved teeth that could crunch through flesh and bones.

Euoplocephalus
(You-op-loh-keff-ah-lus)

Heads or tails?

Plant-eating dinosaurs had to defend themselves from the fierce meat-eaters. *Triceratops* had a heavy, bony head-shield and impressive horns. *Euoplocephalus* swung the bony club at the end of its tail to knock out its enemies. *Iguanodon* may have hit out with its spiked thumb.

Tail of
Euoplocephalus

Thumb
spike of *Iguanodon*

Marvellous mums

All dinosaurs laid eggs like birds. Some baby dinosaurs were able to run about soon after hatching. Others, such as *Maiasaura* (My-ah-sore-ah), needed to be looked after for some time by their mothers.

Look for me

My name is *Psittacosaurus* (Sit-ah-co-sore-us). I am having a snooze near the exit to the gallery. When you find me ask yourself 'Were dinosaurs like animals living today?'

Where did dinosaurs go?

Dinosaurs ruled the Earth for 150 million years. They all disappeared 65 million years ago. What do you think finished them off? It could have been gas and chemicals from volcanoes, or a gigantic asteroid hitting Earth from space.

Human Biology

Time to learn what makes you tick!

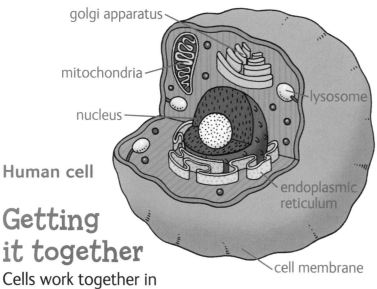

golgi apparatus

mitochondria

nucleus

lysosome

endoplasmic reticulum

cell membrane

Human cell

Getting it together

Cells work together in groups, called tissues. Muscle is one kind of tissue. Each muscle cell is long and thin. Within the cell are minute strands that contract and relax. Many bundles of muscle cells make up each muscle.

What is the smallest part of you?

Like other living things, the smallest part of your body is a single cell. Your body has 50 million, million cells! There are many different cells, such as muscle and nerve cells. Most cells have a nucleus that holds strands of DNA containing sets of instructions, called genes. One set of genes is what makes your eyes brown or blue.

A long strand of DNA

Making a baby

A new life begins when the dad's sperm meets the mum's egg inside her womb. The fertilized egg divides many times, making more and more cells. Gradually, the baby starts to grow. After seven months, the baby looks like this. It will be another two months before the baby is born.

what sound can you hear in our giant-sized womb?

Model of baby inside the womb

Look at the display about joints. What kind of joint lets you bend at the knees?

Pulling power

Your muscles can only pull on your bones. They cannot push them. When you bend your arm, the biceps muscle is pulling. To straighten your arm, the triceps muscle is pulling.

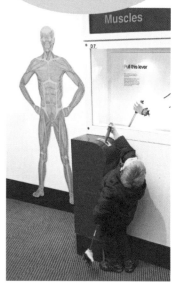

Muscles

Brilliant brain

A human brain is amazing. While you read this, it is taking signals from your eyes and making sense of them. When you turn the page, the brain sends signals along the nerves to trigger the muscles in your hand.

A real human brain and spinal cord

Motor skills

This strange model shows how much of the brain is used to control the movement of different parts of the body. The hands are huge because a large part of the brain is used to control their movement. This is one reason why you can hold a pencil and text on a mobile phone.

Don't forget to try out the memory games in the gallery.

What is memory?

Elephants are supposed never to forget things. Some people may try to remember things by tying a knot in a handkerchief. How do you remember things? Do you write things down or repeat words in your head? A good memory means we can both learn and remember.

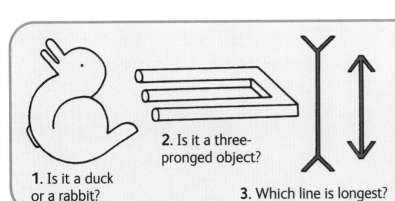

1. Is it a duck or a rabbit?

2. Is it a three-pronged object?

3. Which line is longest?

What do you see?

Your brain tries to make sense of the things you see, using memories of what you have seen before. Sometimes, it can get very confused! Look for these and other eye teasers in the gallery.

Mammals

See marvellous mammals from the present and the past.

Long-tailed macaques

What is a mammal?

Mammal mothers suckle their young on milk. Mammals have a variety of lifestyles from high-flying bats to deep-diving whales. Most mammals have fur or hair. They usually sweat to keep themselves cool. You are a mammal.

Egg-layer

The platypus and echidnas lay eggs instead of giving birth to live young.

The bill-like snout of the platypus can detect electrical signals from worms, snails and other small prey in streams.

Three-banded armadillo

In the pouch

Kangaroos carry their young in a pouch. When it is born, the joey (the baby kangaroo) is the size of a jelly bean. The tiny baby crawls into the pouch where it suckles.

what is the proper name for a mammal that has a pouch?

M _ _ _ U _ _ _ _

Bottoms up

The three-banded armadillo has body armour made of bony plates. When danger approaches, it rolls up into a ball. The fairy armadillo only has bony plates on its back. It escapes danger by burrowing but leaves its bottom sticking out, so the bony plates block the entrance to the burrow.

Fairy armadillo

Sloth

African grassland

Jerboa

Himalayan mountains

South American swamp

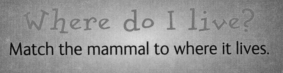

Where do I live?

Match the mammal to where it lives.

Lion

Snow leopard

South American rainforest

Capybara

Sahara desert

Are mammals dying out today?

Mammals are still threatened by over-hunting and destruction of their homes in the wild. Another major threat is climate change which may also destroy wild places. For example, polar bears are in danger of losing their icy hunting grounds as the Arctic ice melts.

What big teeth!

The sabre-toothed cat used its dagger-like teeth to bite into its prey. This cat died out at the end of the last Ice Age about 10,000 years ago.

Mammals

Meet the blue whale and other magnificent mammals.

Count my toes

Many plant-eating mammals have hooves instead of claws. Some of these mammals have two or four toes, which are even numbers. Giraffes, deer and sheep all have two toes. Others have one or three toes which are odd numbers.

Odds on

Fit the names of these odd-toed hoofed mammals into the puzzle: Donkey, Horse, Rhinoceros, Tapir, Zebra

P
N

Climb the stairs to get the best view of the blue whale.

Even-toed mammals

How do large mammals support their weight?

Heavy land mammals, such as elephants and rhinoceroses, have pillar-like legs with big foot pads to support their weight. Whales can grow so large because the water supports their weight. They are crushed by their own weight if they come ashore.

Stand on our scales to find out how many times heavier an elephant is compared to you!

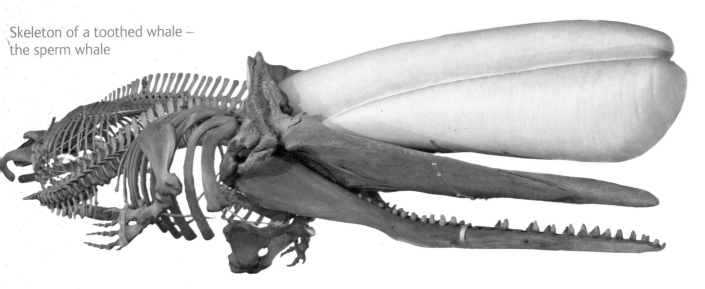

Skeleton of a toothed whale – the sperm whale

What is a whale?

Whales have flippers and a tail fin, called a fluke. The front limb bones support the flippers. The tail fluke has no bones. Some whales, called baleen whales, have bristly plates in their mouths to catch food. Other whales and dolphins have teeth instead.

Bristly plates of a baleen whale

Blue giant

The blue whale is the largest animal that ever lived. It is bigger than the largest dinosaur. The blue whale can weigh up to 150 tonnes. Our famous blue whale was modelled on a beached whale so it not as sleek as the living animal.

Echoes

The toothed whales and dolphins can sense what is around them using sound. They send out high-pitched sounds, which bounce off things in front of them. The time it takes for the echoes to come back tells the whale or dolphin how far away something is.

Fishes, Amphibians and Reptiles

King mackerel

Get to know some weird and wonderful cold-blooded creatures.

What is a fish?

Fishes have fins, live in water and take in oxygen through their gills. Bony fishes usually have scales and their gills are covered by a flap. Sharks have gill slits and gristle-like cartilage instead of bone. There are more kinds of fishes than all the other animals with backbones put together.

Jaws!

Sharks have rows of teeth. When the front ones drop out, they are replaced by the new ones in the row behind. The tiger shark has teeth for cutting and crunching to cope with its diet, which can be almost anything from turtles to sea birds.

Fishy fun

Look at the fishes in the gallery to help you solve the crossword puzzle. Use a pencil so you can rub out any mistakes as some clues have more than one correct answer!

1. What fish has a pointed weapon on its snout?
2. What kind of fish breathes air?
3. What fish can blow itself up into a prickly balloon?
4. What deep-sea fish has a huge mouth?
5. What deep-sea fish has a very long fishing rod on its head?
6. What fish fathers give birth?
7. What fish walks along the seabed?

Tiger shark jaws

What is an amphibian?

Frogs, salamanders and newts are among the different kinds of amphibians. The adults live on land but lay their eggs in water or damp places. Most adult amphibians have lungs but they all breathe through their skins.

You can find out about the largest reptiles that ever lived on land and in the sea on pages 5, 7 and 20.

What is a reptile?

Turtles, tortoises, snakes, lizards and crocodiles are all reptiles. They have dry scaly skins and usually lay eggs on land. Many kinds of reptiles bask in the sun to warm up.

Shrinking frog

When frogs lay eggs in water the eggs hatch into tadpoles. This paradoxical frog is unusual because the tadpole is much larger than the adult frog. The tadpole's large tail disappears when the tadpole turns into a frog.

Tortoises have a bony shell covered in horny scales

Can you spot the differences between a sea turtle and a land tortoise?

Slithery snakes

Snakes are legless reptiles that have a long bendy backbone. As they slither along their body makes S bends. Some snakes use venom to subdue their prey. Others, such as pythons, kill by coiling around their victims and squeezing tight.

How can you tell a crocodile from an alligator?

Nile crocodile

Stomach contents

Model of Komodo dragon

Never smile at a crocodile

The Nile crocodile has powerful jaws armed with sharp pointed teeth. They cannot chew, but tear off chunks of flesh instead. The beads and bangle on display may have been swallowed to help the crocodile grind up food in its stomach. Do you think a person was wearing them at the time?

Beastly bite

Growing much bigger than a large dog, the Komodo dragon is the largest lizard living today. The dragon lives on islands in Indonesia. Its saliva is full of bacteria so that if a person or animal is bitten, they may die from blood poisoning.

Marine Invertebrates

Dive in to see spineless wonders from the sea.

What is a marine invertebrate?

Marine invertebrates (in-ver-ter-brate) are spineless animals that live in the sea. Many kinds of sea animals do not have backbones. Corals, clams, crabs, snails, starfish and sponges are just some of these animals.

Meet our scientists daily in the Attenborough Studio.

Skeleton of stony coral

Stingers

Corals have stinging tentacles like their relatives, the jellyfish and anemones. These animals are called cnidaria (nye-dare-ree-ah). Living corals are made up of thousands of tiny anemone-like individuals. In reef-building corals, each individual makes a stony cup to protect itself.

Not in my bath

You can use a natural bath sponge to keep you clean. Barrel sponges are too hard to bathe with. Sponges are simple animals with no nerves, muscles or other tissues. They take in water and filter out particles of food.

Barrel sponge

You can see more crustaceans in Creepy Crawlies.

Cutting and crushing

Lobsters have one pincer for crushing snails, clams and the like. The other pincer snips up the flesh. Lobsters have two pairs of feelers and four pairs of walking legs. All crustaceans (crust-ay-shuns) have two pairs of feelers.

Should you buy sea souvenirs?

It is tempting to buy pretty shells, corals and other souvenirs. But how do you know if there will be enough left in the sea for the future? Bringing home some souvenirs, such as corals, is against the law.

Deadly beauties

If you visit a tropical reef, never pick a cone shell up. Some kinds of cone snails have a deadly sting. Snails, clams and squid are some of the soft-bodied animals that we call molluscs (moll-usks).

If you are 8 or over take the *Spirit Collection Tour* to see a real giant squid.

Model of a giant squid

Giant of the deep

The giant squid has eyes the size of dinner plates to help it to see in the ocean depths. Only a little light filters from the surface to where the giant squid lives at about 600 metres down, which is about 300 times the depth of an Olympic swimming pool.

Reef watch

Can you find seven spineless animals on this reef apart from corals? Don't count the fishes, they have backbones!

Creepy Crawlies

Spot creepy crawlies on land, in water and in your home.

What is an arthropod?

Animals that creep about on jointed legs are called arthropods (ar-thro-pods). They do not have a backbone like you. Instead, their skeleton is on the outside like a suit of armour. Arthropods have to split open their skeleton to grow larger.

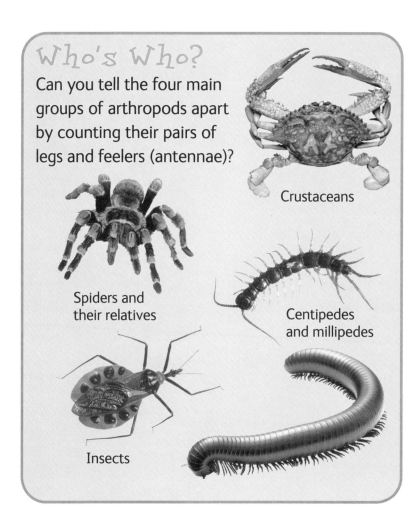

Who's Who?

Can you tell the four main groups of arthropods apart by counting their pairs of legs and feelers (antennae)?

Crustaceans

Spiders and their relatives

Centipedes and millipedes

Insects

Webs worldwide

Many spiders weave webs to catch their prey. The male spider may pluck on the strands to make sure the female knows not to eat him. Try your luck in our spider mating game in the gallery.

Our model is many times larger than a real scorpion!

Sting in the tail

Like spiders, scorpions have four pairs of legs for walking. They grab prey with their pincers. The tail swings down over the head and the sting is used to stun their prey or enemy.

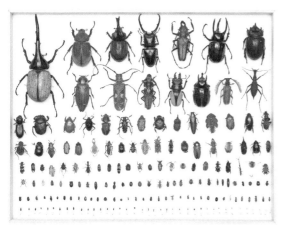

Why are there so many insects?

Insects are the largest group of animals with over one million different kinds. Most insects are smaller than a 10 pence coin so there are many places where they can live. Can you think of other reasons why there are so many different kinds?

Long legs

The Japanese spider crab is the largest living arthropod. Its long legs are used to walk across the sea floor. When stretched out the legs measure up to four metres across.

All change

Some insects go through a complete change when they grow up. A butterfly's egg hatches into a caterpillar. When fully grown, the caterpillar becomes a chrysalis. Inside the chrysalis, the caterpillar turns into a butterfly.

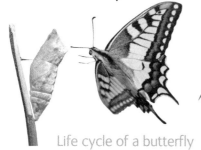

Life cycle of a butterfly

Look for more crabs in the *Marine Invertebrates* gallery.

Watch our leafcutters online at www.nhm.ac.uk/ kids-only/ naturecams

Ant maze

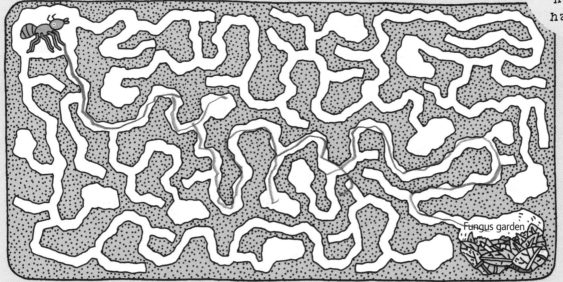

Fungus garden

Leafcutter ants grow fungus on chewed leaves. Can you get our ant to its garden?

Fossil Marine Reptiles

Look up at the gallery walls to see fossils of monsters from the deep.

You can see a rebuilt ichthyosaur skeleton in the Central Hall.

What are giant marine reptiles?

Giant reptiles swam in the sea when dinosaurs roamed the land. Like all reptiles, these marine reptiles breathed air so they had to swim to the surface of the sea every so often.

Sea worthy

Ichthyosaurs had a dolphin-like shape but they swam like fish with a sideways sweep of their tails. They also had two pairs of flippers for steering. The fin on their back stopped them rolling in the water.

Tail first

This fossil of an ichthyosaur mother shows her four babies. When the mother died, three of the babies were still inside her and the fourth had just been born tail first.

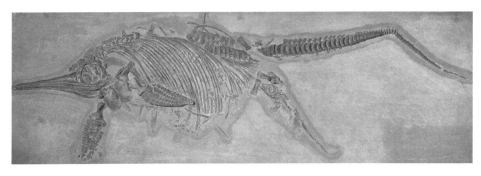

Can you see the baby ichthyosaur (ick-thee-oh-sore) being born?

Pliosaur (ply-oh-sore)

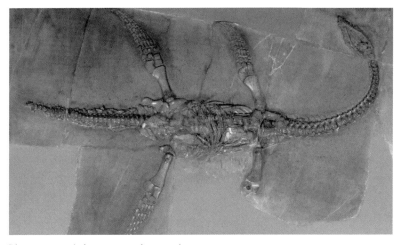

Long or short necks?

Plesiosaurs had small heads and long necks. The pliosaurs had bigger heads and usually shorter necks. Both swam along using their paddle-shaped limbs to propel themselves through the water. They died out at the same time as the dinosaurs.

Plesiosaur (plee-zee-oh-sore)

Old croc

This fossil sea crocodile lived around 180 million years ago. It caught fish with its needle-shaped teeth. Like today's saltwater crocodiles, it may have lived at the mouth of a river and swum along the coast to new places.

Sea crocodile

Can you find dinosaur fossils in this gallery?

Mosasaur

Another biggie

Mosasaurs swam in the ancient seas after the ichthyosaurs had already died out. They became extinct at the same time as the dinosaurs. Mosasaurs had huge teeth and were longer than a double-decker bus.

Find the fossil

Join the dots to find a giant marine reptile.

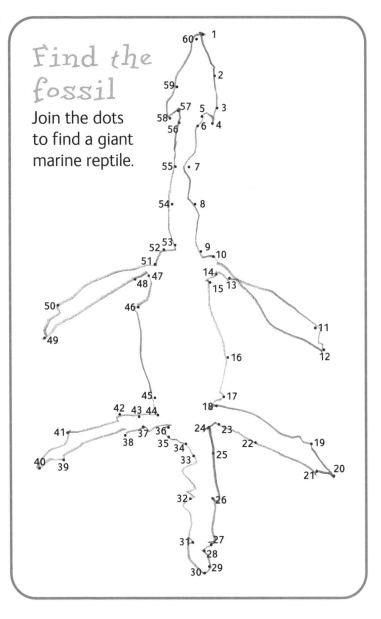

Fossil hunter

Mary Anning (1799-1847) was a whizz at finding fossils of giant marine reptiles near her home on the south coast of England. She was only 11 years old when she found her first ichthyosaur.

Birds

Seek out your finest feathered friends.

Toucan can fly

Ostrich cannot fly

What is a bird?

Birds have feathers, wings and lay hard-shelled eggs. Most birds can fly although penguins use their wings to swim instead. Some birds, such as the ostrich and cassowary, only have tiny wings so cannot fly.

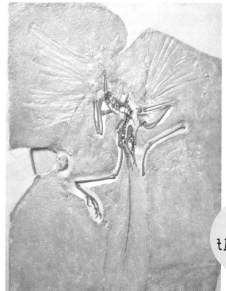

Early bird

Archaeopteryx (Ar-kee-op-ter-iks) is the earliest known bird. It lived around 147 million years ago. This peculiar bird had teeth and a long bony tail like a reptile. Unlike its feathered dinosaur ancestors, *Archaeopteryx* was able to fly.

You can see a replica of this precious fossil in the gallery

Beaks and feet

Birds of prey, such as owls, have a hooked beak for tearing flesh and sharp talons for grabbing prey.

Can you work out what other birds do by looking at their beak and feet?

Neat nests

Birds make their nests out of all kinds of stuff. The cave swiftlet makes a nest out of its spit. People collect the nests to make into soup. This weaver bird's grass nest has a long funnel-shaped entrance to stop snakes getting inside to steal the eggs.

Little and large

Hummingbirds lay the smallest eggs in the world. The ostrich lays the largest egg, weighing over one and a half kilos, which is about the weight of 25 chickens' eggs.

Hummingbird egg

Ostrich egg

Bright and beautiful

You can see hundreds of hummingbirds and their nests. The birds' shiny colours come from light bouncing off tiny layers inside some of their feathers. In the 1800s displays like these were fashionable.

Why are birds colourful?

Male birds of many different kinds have bright and colourful feathers which may help to attract a partner or alert an intruder that a territory is occupied. Females often have duller colours which make it harder for predators to spot them on their nest.

Colour me in

Colour in the peacock or make a note of his colours to fill in later.

Can you find a dodo on the walls inside the Museum?

Dead as a dodo

The flightless dodo was an easy target for sailors who stopped off on the Indian Ocean island of Mauritius from the late 1500s. The sailors left pigs and rats behind that destroyed the dodos' nests and eggs. Within a hundred years, the dodo was wiped out.

Ecology

Explore what connects all living things.

What is ecology?

Ecology is the study of how living things interact with each other and the world around them. Some live on land while others live in rivers, lakes or the sea. Whether on land or in water, almost all living things rely on energy from the sun.

Water for life

Every living thing needs water, which is recycled all the time. The sun's heat draws water from the sea. The water turns into clouds and then it rains. The water runs into rivers and goes back to the sea. When you pee, you are recycling water!

The leaf factory

Imagine you have shrunk down 8,000 times and can fit inside a leaf! Green chemicals capture energy from sunlight to help the leaf make food from carbon dioxide. In doing so, the leaf lets out oxygen, which we all need to breathe.

Tigers are meat-eaters

Meat or veg?

Plants make their own food so are at the start of the food chain. Plant-eating animals are the next link in the chain. The plant-eaters are eaten in turn by meat-eaters. Sometimes, even the meat-eaters are eaten by other meat-eaters.

Sloths are plant-eaters

How can you help the planet?

Humans have the greatest impact of all living things on the planet. There are over six billion of us. We use up much of the Earth's resources from fish in the sea to oil underground. The changes we make often harm the planet.

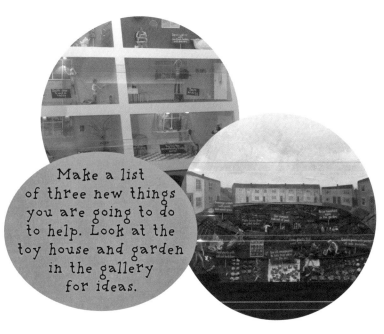

Make a list of three new things you are going to do to help. Look at the toy house and garden in the gallery for ideas.

Link us up

Can you number these living things in their correct order in the food chain?

Recycled rabbit

Have you ever thought what happens to dead stuff and dung? It is food for other living things, such as fungi and bacteria. These decomposers break down the material and release nutrients into the soil. The nutrients are then taken up by plants so they get recycled.

You can visit our *Wildlife Garden* except in winter.

Go wild

Our Wildlife Garden gives wild animals and plants somewhere to live in the city. We have places where different kinds of wildlife can live including a pond, meadow, hedgerow, heath and woodland.

Primates

Hang out with some of your closest relatives.

Who are you?

Primates are mammals. You are a primate! You belong to the group of primates, called apes. Other apes are gibbons, orang-utans and chimpanzees. All apes (and some monkeys too) have fingernails and toenails like you. They are able to rotate their thumb opposite the fingers as you can do.

Orang-utan

What is a primate?

Primates have hands and feet that can grasp, which means they can climb trees and hang onto branches. Their eyes face forward so they can spot things in front of them and judge distances well. Most primates have nails instead of claws.

Find the primates

Can you find the names of these primates in the word search?

AYEAYE, BUSHBABY
CHIMPANZEE, GIBBON
GORILLA, LEMUR
LORIS, MONKEY
ORANGUTAN
POTTO, TARSIER

```
                    Z R
                    H Z
                  D H E E
                  P E X S
                N O B B I G
                Z M R Y D O
  U G O R I L L A B E Q E J G L E M U R S
  D B H O I P A O U I D Y W O E E Y G L C
  D Z W S U N N S S K A L M X Z V Z G
  N O J S T H H R M E O L N N C T
    K F K Y S B A N Y R X A A U
    O R G M A T G A I E T P
  W A T O Q B N F L S B U M V
    P K N T K Y Q B X W E G I O
  S Q K E W O Q G Q T T M N H H Q
  M E P Y V K P     Y C S A C X G
  P Y Y R X H M     Y S R P T S G
  J W A V C         O O V N D
  U K T Y                   Y K M L
  V A                       H B
```

Social skills

Some primates live by themselves, such as the potto. Many others, such as squirrel monkeys and chimpanzees, live in groups. A chimp may signal to others in its group by making faces and different calls.

which of these chimps is making a threat and which is frightened?

Bright and brainy

We pride ourselves on being brainy. But did you know some primates can do clever things too? Chimpanzees can use simple tools, such as a twig to get tasty termites out of a nest. They also seem to understand simple sentences made of symbols.

Bringing up baby

Baby primates are helpless when born so have to be cared for by their parents. Grasping hands help a baby to cling onto its mum. Baby apes take a long time to grow up with us humans having the longest childhood.

Chimpanzee
mother
and baby

Model of a
Neanderthal
woman

Why are primates in danger?

The giant lemur and 13 other kinds of lemurs died out after people first arrived on the island of Madagascar about 2,000 years ago. Today, many primates are also at a risk as people eat them and cut down the forests where they live.

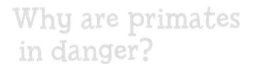

Giant lemur
skull

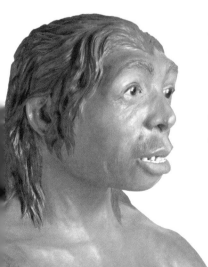

How we came to be

Modern humans like us evolved at least 195,000 years ago. We are survivors whereas our closest relatives, including the Neanderthals, died out. Today, chimpanzees and bonobos are our closest living relatives.

Minerals and The Vault

Admire minerals, meteorites, gemstones and jewels.

Graphite pencil

Graphite mineral

What is a mineral?

A mineral is a natural material of a particular chemical composition and crystal structure. Most rocks are made of several different kinds of mineral. For example, granite is a common rock that is chiefly made up of quartz and feldspar minerals.

Structure counts

The lead in your pencils is a soft mineral, called graphite. The hardest mineral is diamond. Both graphite and diamond are made of pure carbon but their crystal structure is different.

Diamond

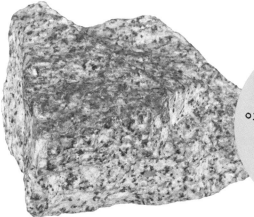

Find the granite in the open display of rocks. Can you see crystals of clear quartz and white feldspar?

A large part of the *Minerals* gallery is a scientific display of minerals in the original Victorian cases.

Animal, vegetable or mineral?

Some substances made by living things are minerals. Stony corals make their skeletons out of the mineral calcite. Chalk is mostly calcite too. But it is made from the skeletons of tiny plant-like organisms that sank to the bottom of ancient seas.

Chalk cliffs made of tiny plant-like organisms

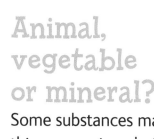

Giant gem

Gemstones are beautiful minerals. They are often cut into shapes to show off their colour and sparkle. This topaz, our largest cut stone, is about the size of a pack of cards.

You can see valuable specimens and rare meteorites in *The Vault.* Do you dare look there for the cursed amethyst?

What is a meteorite?

A meteorite is a rock from space that hits the Earth. Most meteorites are fragments of giant rocks, called asteroids. More rarely, meteorites may have come from the moon or Mars.

Lunar meteorite

Iron meteorite

You can see a wealth of gems and precious metals in the *Earth's Treasury.*

Count the gems

See if you can find...
5 diamonds
2 emeralds
1 amethyst
2 rubies
3 sapphires

Gold rush

This gold nugget was found in 1853 during the Australian gold rush. Most gold is worn smooth after it has been carried away by rivers. Gold is rarely found with cube-shaped crystals like these.

Butterscotch crystals

Crystals often form in spaces inside rocks. Here, minerals are able to grow into fantastic shapes. These wulfenite crystals are the colour of butterscotch.

Earth Hall

Wonder at our visions of the Earth.

Lodestone acts like a magnet and attracts metal pins

Finding the way

Early sailors navigated by the position of the stars. Over a thousand years ago, simple compasses were invented with iron needles that pointed north. The needle was magnetized by rubbing it against a naturally magnetic rock called a lodestone.

What is the Earth?

The Earth is one of eight planets that revolve around our star, the sun. In ancient times, people thought the sun revolved around the Earth. People knew little about space or even the rocks on Earth.

What other striking minerals or rocks can you find in the Earth Hall?

Malachite is a copper mineral that was once added to paint to give it a green colour

A marvelous mineral

Malachite is a bright green mineral that grows like a bunch of grapes, or like a stalagmite. It is a soft stone. When it is cut and polished it is one of the most beautiful gemstones, which is why it is often used for ornaments and jewellery.

Rich resource

Iron has shaped our history from its first use in simple tools to the elegant steel bridges of today. The kidney-shaped ore you see here is 70 per cent iron. Such rich sources of iron are rare.

Discover spectacular objects in the round windows!

Devil's toenails

In the past, people thought these fossils of extinct oysters were the devil's toenails. They had no idea that seashells could be preserved in the rocks as fossils.

Moon rock

Our moon revolves around the Earth. The piece of moon rock inside this pyramid was brought to Earth in 1972. It is part of a 5.5 kilogramme boulder collected from the surface of the moon by US astronauts on the Apollo 16 mission.

word scramble

Help, our printer has gone haywire! Can you unscramble the words in our labels in the Earth Hall?

LSOFSI
OALCR
MTEESNOG
AYSCRTL
LMNIAER

What is the future of the Earth?

We know more about the Earth than ever before. Yet we still have much to learn about how to use its resources wisely. Visit *Earth Today and Tomorrow* to find out how our planet is coping.

Cars are now crushed and recycled

Volcanoes and Earthquakes

Feel the forces within the Earth.

What is a volcano?

Deep within the Earth is molten rock and gas, called magma. When magma finds cracks in the surface rocks, it forces its way out as a volcano where temperatures can reach over 1,150°C. Some volcanoes are quiet for many years then erupt dramatically. Others spew out molten rock at frequent intervals.

> **Magma or lava?** Magma and lava are both molten rock. When magma reaches the surface, it is called lava.

Hair of a goddess

People from the Pacific Ocean island of Hawaii once believed that these strands were the hair of their volcano goddess Pele. The strands actually formed from erupting lava that has been caught by the wind.

Light as a rock!

Some molten volcanic rock is rich in gas. When it reaches the surface, the gas expands to make a rocky froth. On cooling, the froth is turned into a solid rock full of air holes, called pumice.

> Silky smooth to touch this mineral-like rock is hard and breaks very easily.

Lifting pumice

Nature's glass

When lava cools rapidly, its minerals have no time to form crystals. The sharp, glassy rock made is called obsidian (ob-sid-ee-an).

Vesuvius' victims

In AD 79 Mount Vesuvius in Italy erupted showering the town of Pompeii below with an avalanche of hot ash and rocks. The bodies of some victims were preserved in hardened ash. By filling the cavities left by the bodies with plaster, we can see what they looked like when they died.

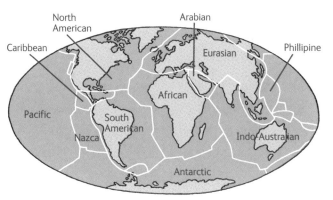

Moving plates

The Earth is made of gigantic plates that take millions of years to drift across its surface. In some places, such as along the floor of the Atlantic Ocean, molten rock comes out and forces the plates apart. In other places, plates collide and one may move under the other, down into the Earth's molten interior.

What is an earthquake?

Earthquakes are the shaking forces that mostly come from movements of the Earth's plates. In March 2011, an earthquake hit Japan's northeast coast. Sadly, 15,370 people were killed as buildings fell down and as the tsunami, triggered by the earthquake, swept over the land.

Experience the earthquake – the force of the real quake would be many times greater

Earth quiz

1. What are the giant waves caused by a volcano or an earthquake called?
a. Tide
b. Tsunami
c. Surf

2. How is pillow lava made?
a. By stuffing feathers into a pillow case
b. By the wind cooling lumps of molten lava
c. By lava cooling under the sea

3. What happens if magma cools slowly?
a. Large crystals form in the rock
b. Small crystals form in the rock
c. No crystals form in the rock

4. What is someone who studies a volcano called?
a. Palaeontologist
b. Biologist
c. Volcanologist

Restless Surface

Dig into the Earth's ever-changing surface.

What is weathering?

Surface rocks are under constant attack. They can be broken down by acidic chemicals in rain like this limestone gargoyle. They can also be broken up by physical forces. For example, when water in a crack freezes, it expands and may shatter rock.

Gargoyle

How different do these rocks feel to touch?

Do you know the name for a feature growing down from the roof of a cave?

Carried away

Loose rocks are carried away and eroded by water, wind and ice. The odd-shaped rock has been blasted by wind and rain that have removed more of the softer layers. The boulder has been carried in water where its sharp edges were worn away by other rocks as it rolled along.

Rock gouged by a glacier

Mites go up

Over hundreds of years, mineral-rich water dripping onto the floor of a limestone cave makes a stalagmite.

Gouged by ice

The gouges in this rock were made by sharp rock fragments carried by a glacier. The fragments made these deep grooves as the ice moved slowly down a slope.

Patterns in the sand

On the beach you may see how a stream flowing out to sea makes channels in the sand. What patterns can you make in our sand table?

Look for ripple marks made by waves on a sandy beach that have been preserved in stone in Lasting Impressions.

Get sorted

Sand, pebbles and even shells are picked up and carried along by moving water. When the water slows down, it drops the larger material first. Strong currents moved these shells into a heap millions of years ago, then sand and mud dropped on top of them.

Who made the pyramids?

Everyone knows the ancient Egyptians built the pyramids. But did you know the rocks are partly made up of large, single-celled organisms, called nummulites?

Limestone rock showing nummulites (numm-u-lites)

What helps to wear away mountains?

Fill in the puzzle to reveal the answer in the shaded squares.

1. What are rocks made of?
2. What planet do we live on?
3. What fossil fuel is made of woody material?
4. What grows up from the floor of a cave?
5. What expands in cracks to shatter rocks?
6. What do we call life forms turned into rocks?
7. What living animals helped to build the pyramids?

1.   L
2.
3.
4.   M
5.
6.
7. U

Earth's Treasury

Unlock the treasures from the rocks.

Granite

What is a rock?

Rocks come in three main types. Igneous rocks, such as granite, form from molten rock. Sedimentary rocks, such as sandstone, form from other rocks and from the remains of living things and crystallisation of minerals. Lastly, metamorphic rocks such as gneiss are changed by heat and pressure deep within the Earth.

Gneiss

Sandstone

> You can see more glow-in-the-dark minerals outside the *Minerals Gallery* and in the *Earth Hall.*

Superman's super enemy

Our scientists were amazed to discover a new mineral in Serbia that has the same chemical composition as the kryptonite in the film, *Superman Returns*. Kryptonite is the only substance that can weaken Superman. The new mineral is actually called jadarite.

Glow in the dark

We cannot see ultraviolet light (UV). But shine UV light on some kinds of minerals, and you can see them glow in the dark like this fluorite and willemite. The minerals take in UV light then emit the energy in colours you can see.

Diamonds at work

Diamonds are the hardest substance known. Tiny diamonds can be made artificially under great heat and pressure. Diamond powders are used to polish hard rock.

Natural diamond

Synthetic diamond powder

Double vision

Minerals have different properties. If you look through a crystal of the mineral calcite you will see things in double.

As light rays go through the crystal, they are split in two. Try looking through the huge crystal in the gallery.

Fuel from rocks

Oil is the remains of tiny plants and animals that lived in lakes and the sea. The remains sunk to the bottom and were covered by layers of mud and sand. The weight of the layers above turned the remains into oil.

Can you name another type of fossil fuel in the gallery?

Useful metals

Metals taken from the rocks can be made into many things. See if you can fill in the missing words. Can you find the answers in the gallery?

Silver is made into _ _ w _ _ _ _ _ y

Copper is made into _ i _ i _ _

Iron is made into _ _ e e _

Lead is made into r _ _ _ i _ _

Why is sand so useful?

Sand grains are tiny fragments of rock. Sand is mostly made of the common mineral quartz that you see here as a big crystal. Quartz is made of silicon and oxygen. Quartz sand is used to make computer chips, glass, ceramics and sandpaper.

From the Beginning

Trek through time.

Follow the gallery's timeline, each metre equals 25 million years!

How old is the Earth?

Scientists can tell how old the Earth is by studying meteorites. Unlike rocks on Earth, the oldest meteorites have not changed since the solar system was formed. The solar system (including the Earth) is about 4,560 million years old. This meteorite is made of debris left after the solar system formed.

You can find out about meteorites on page 29.

Rock rust

Scientists can find clues about early life on Earth by looking at rocks. The reddish bands in this 3,000 million-year-old rock contain iron combined with oxygen like rust. Scientists believe that the oxygen was made by the Earth's first plant-like organisms.

First life forms

Tiny fossils show that there were chains of simple cells living on Earth 3,500 million years ago.

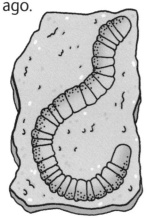

Fossil jigsaw

You have discovered parts of a weird fossil animal in the rocks. Can you put them together correctly?
Clue – *Anomalacaris* (Ano-ma-la-caris), an early arthropod had front legs that grasped its trilobite prey.

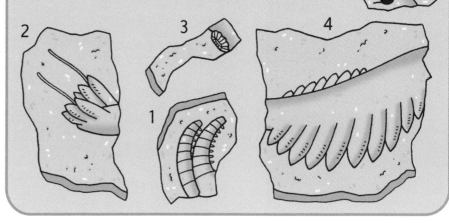

In the sea

Around 545 million years ago, a variety of animals lived in the sea. Some animals were soft and squishy like jellyfish. Others had hard parts such as shells and outer skeletons. Many of these early animals, including trilobites, became extinct 248 million years ago.

Trilobite

Look for trilobites and other sea fossils in *Fossils in Britain and Earth Lab*.

First fishes

The first fishes had no jaws. Around 400 million years ago, fishes with jaws appeared. This huge fish had jaws and lived about 90 million years ago.

Stepping onto land

The first four-legged animals clambered onto land about 375 million years ago. Like amphibians today, they bred in water. Reptiles, like this early plant-eater, were the first to lay eggs on land.

13,000-year-old ground sloth fur and poo

Strange remains

Mammals did well after the dinosaurs died out 65 million years ago. Among the mammals, humans were late arrivals with people like us appearing 160,000 years ago. From about 10,000 years ago, human hunters began to kill off many kinds of large animals including the ground sloth.

You can see the skeleton of another kind of giant sloth at the end of the *Fossil Marine Reptiles* gallery.

Incredible Collections

Stored behind the scenes are all sorts of bizarre and beautiful specimens.

What is in store?

We have over 70 million specimens in store with around 150,000 more added each year. Specimens are kept in the main Museum, the Darwin Centre, our South London Store and the Natural History Museum at Tring.

Our specimens include about ...

28 million insects

27 million other animals

9 million fossils

6 million plants

1 million birds

500,000 rocks and minerals

3,200 meteorites

Sir Hans Sloane

Thanks Sir Hans

Our collections began when a wealthy doctor, Sir Hans Sloane (1660-1753) left 80,000 specimens to the British people. First displayed in the British Museum, the collections were moved to South Kensington in the late 1800s.

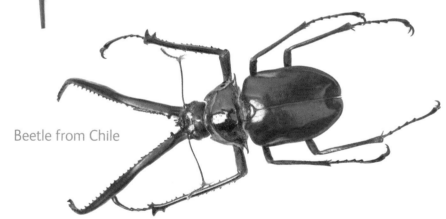

Beetle from Chile

Biting beetle

Charles Darwin (1809-1882) was a famous scientist who put forward ideas of how living things can change through time. We have some of his collections including this beetle from Chile, which nipped his finger.

Flesh-eating beetle

We use flesh-eating beetles and their larvae to strip bones for storage. See them at www. nhm.ac.uk/kids-only/nature cams.

Wet, dry and frozen

Some of our animal specimens are kept in jars of fluid. Others are kept dry, such as shells, skeletons and skins. We also keep frozen tissue and DNA from endangered animals. If one of these became extinct, the frozen material would give us valuable information about the animal.

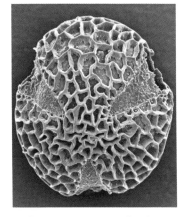

Pollen grain magnified many times lifesize

Whale bones in the South London Store

Little and large

Pollen grains are some of the tiniest things in store. They are usually kept on microscope slides. The largest specimen in store is a blue whale skeleton, but it is not as large as the one you can see in the *Mammals* gallery.

State of the art facilities

Collections, scientists and visitors come together in the *Darwin Centre*, the exciting new wing of the Museum. It houses the animal, plant and insect collections, and high-tech science labs. You can see the scientists at work and take a closer look at the collections.

Preparing a dinosaur bone

Set in stone

Our experts get fossils out of solid rock. First, they remove bits of rock with a hammer and chisel. Then they may use acids or fire hard pellets at the rock. Finally, they remove the last grains of rock using a dentist's drill, scalpels and needles.

If you are 8 years or older, you can go on a tour to see some of our animal specimens in the *Darwin Centre*.

A giant insect cocoon under glass

Super Science

Our scientists are discovering more about the natural world.

What do our scientists do?

The Museum has over 350 scientists. They study the collections to understand the variety of life. New species are discovered by comparing specimens with those already identified in our collections.

Collecting specimens from the top of the forest

First Brits

Our scientists led the team that discovered early people lived in Britain over 800,000 years ago. When ice sheets covered Britain, these early peoples either died out or moved south. Others then returned when it was warmer. About 12,000 years ago, our ancestors were able to settle in Britain for good.

Martian meteorites

The Museum has 12 fragments of some 75 Martian meteorites that have been discovered on Earth. Studying the meteorites gives us clues as to what Mars was like in the past.

Go to page 29 to find out more about meteorites.

What is a person who studies meteorites called? Meteorologist or meteoriticist

Deadly diseases

Tiny worms infect over 200 million people. If an infected person pees or poos in a lake, the worms can be picked up by snails. The worms multiply in the snails and when shed into the water can infect other people. Museum scientists are studying the worms and snails to find ways to control them.

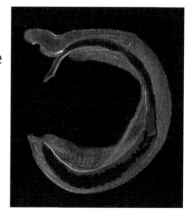

Worm parasite

Tracking mozzies

Certain kinds of mosquitoes carry malaria, which is a disease that kills over one million people each year. Our scientists are finding a new way to identify the dangerous mosquitoes by identifying bits of their DNA (genes).

Forest finds

Three new kinds of salamander were discovered on an expedition to explore a forest reserve in Costa Rica, South America. Scientists from the Museum are helping to record the amazing variety of plants and animals in the reserve.

Stranded whales

The Museum records whales and dolphins that have come ashore around Britain. Some have died at sea before being washed up on the beach. Others have swum ashore by mistake and then died. Sadly, many whales and dolphins die after being caught in fishing gear.

Plant protection

The xaté (sha-tay) palm is used in flower arrangements because the cut stems last for a long time. Museum scientists helped to find ways to protect the palm, which is illegally harvested from forests in Belize, South America.

Come and be a scientist in the *Investigate Centre*. Use microscopes and other scientific tools to explore hundreds of stunning objects from the natural world in the same way that our Museum scientists do.

More about the Museum

Discover more fascinating facts.

Is it real?

Not all the specimens you see in our displays are real. Some are models or casts made from the real thing. Soft parts are usually removed because they rot. So you can see dry bones, shells and stuffed specimens. Some fishes are stuffed too, others are models or pickled in fluid.

Coelacanth (see-la-canth)

Spot the real bits

Look at the hippopotamus model in the *Mammals* gallery. Which bits of the hippo are real?

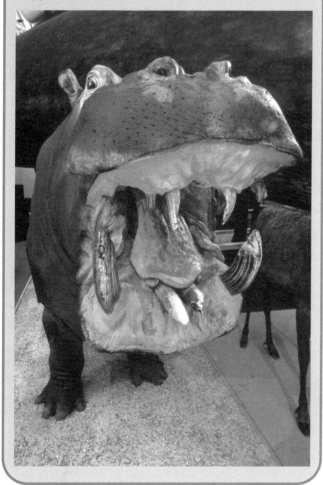

Old collections

Most of the animals you see in the Museum were collected many years ago. This is why some of them look faded. Today, we do not take animals from the wild just for a display. Some of the animals are now endangered, such as the black rhinoceros.

Black rhino collected many years ago

Dust busters

Over the years, dust settles on anything not kept inside a case. We have a team of dust busters who keep our specimens clean. They use special vacuum cleaners, dusters and brushes. One of their biggest jobs is to clean the blue whale.

On paper

Our libraries have over six million books, papers on science, notebooks, maps and artworks. This sketch of a kangaroo made in 1770 was drawn during Captain James Cook's voyage to Australia. It was the first picture of a kangaroo made by a person from Europe.

Party time

When the last visitor has left for the day, the Museum is not as quiet as you may think. On some nights, huge parties are held in the *Central Hall*. Parties help us to raise money to help support the Museum's work.

Saving energy

The Museum is trying to help the planet by using less energy. We have a new power plant that uses waste heat from electricity generation to keep the Museum warm. Meters keep a check on how much electricity is used on every floor.

Answers

p2 Q: *What other features make it look like a cathedral?* A: Pillars, stained glass, high ceiling, gilded panels.

p2 Q: *How many of these clay creatures can you spot inside and outside the Museum?* Bat (top of some pillars in the *Ecology* gallery and Museum Shop); kangaroo (above the Museum's main entrance); lion (roof on the left wing as you face the entrance); monkey (on the arches in the Central Hall); octopus (near the bottom of some pillars in the *Dinosaurs* gallery); owl (on the top of some pillars in the *Dinosaurs* gallery - best seen from the walkway); Pterosaur (outside on the right wing as you face the entrance).

p3 Q: *The tree was a seedling in AD 557. How old was the tree when it was cut down in 1892?* A: The redwood was cut down when it was 1,335 years old!

p5 *Allosaurus, Baryonyx, Coelophysis, Deinocheirus, Edmontosaurus, Fukuiraptor, Gallimimus, Hypsilophodon, Iguanodon, Janenschia, Khaan, Lycorhinus, Maiasaurus, Nomingia, Oviraptor, Pachycephalosaurus, Quaesitosaurus, Rugops, Saltopus, Tyrannosaurus, Utahraptor, Velociraptor, Wannanosaurus, Xenoposeidon, Yinlong, Zalmoxes*

p6 Match the heads
A: A, *Oviraptor*; B, *Baryonyx*; C, *Euoplocephalus*

p8 Q: *What sound can you hear in our giant-sized womb?* A: You can hear the mum's heart beat.

p8 Q: *What kind of joint lets you bend at the knees?* A: A hinge joint.

p9 Q: *What do you see?* A: 1. You may see this as both a duck and a rabbit. 2. The lines drawn trick our brain as only parts of the object are in 3D. 3. Both lines are the same length.

p10 Q: *What is the proper name for a mammal that has a pouch?* A: Marsupial.

p11 Q: *Match the mammal to where it lives.* A: Sloth, South American rainforest; jerboa, Sahara desert; lion, African grassland; capybara, South American swamp; snow leopard, Himalayan mountains.

p12 Odds on
Q: *Fill in the names of some odd-toed hoofed mammals.*

p14 Fishy fun

p15 Spot the difference A: Sea turtles, such as the leatherback turtle, have flattened shells, which make them more streamlined, and flippers. Tortoises have domed shells and legs for walking.

p15 Q: *How can you tell a crocodile from an alligator?* A: When the crocodile's jaws are shut, you can see the fourth tooth in its lower jaw. In the alligator (and caiman) the tooth is hidden because the fourth tooth slots into a pit in the upper jaw.

p17 Q: *Can you find 7 spineless animals apart from corals on this coral reef?* A: Jellyfish; cone snail; giant clam; lobster; starfish; sea urchin; sea anemone.

p18 Q: *Can you tell the four main groups of arthropods apart by counting their pairs of legs and feelers (antennae)?* A: Spiders and their relatives have four pairs of legs and no feelers. Crustaceans have two pairs of feelers. Centipedes have one pair of legs on each segment of their body and millipedes have two pairs of legs on each segment. Millipedes usually have more pairs of legs than centipedes but never have 1,000 legs. They have one pair of feelers. Insects have three pairs of legs and one pair of feelers.

p19 Q: *Why are there so many insects?* A: Insects live in freshwater, on land and in the sea. Insects do not need to eat much to stay alive. Insects breed quickly and can adapt to new conditions.

**p19
Ant maze**

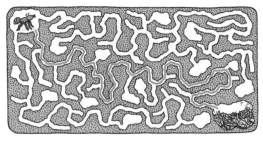

p21 Q: *Can you find dinosaur fossils in this gallery?*
A: Plesiosaurs, ichthyosaurs and other giant marine reptiles were not dinosaurs. Did you spot the slab of rock with a fossil *Stegosaurus* dinosaur in this gallery?

p21 Find the fossil
A: The pliosaur *Rhomaleosaurus*, which has a long neck.

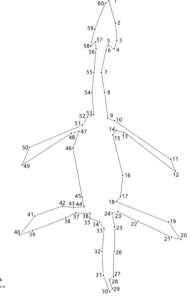

p23 Q: *Can you find a dodo on the walls of the Museum?*
A: In the *Minerals* gallery above a door to the left of *The Vault*.

p25 Link us up
A: 1. Sun; 2. oak leaf; 3. caterpillar; 4. blue tit; 5. hawk.

p26 Find the primates

```
          Z R
          H Z
        D H E E
        P E X S
      N O B B I G
      Z M R Y D O
U G O R I L L A B E Q E J G L E M U R S
D B H O I P A O U I D Y W O E E Y G L C
D Z W S U N N S S K A L M X Z V Z G
  N O J S T H H R M E O L N N C T
  K F K Y S B A N Y R X A A U
    O R G M A T G A I E T P
  W A T O Q B N F L S B U M V
  P K N T K Y Q B X W E G I O
S Q K E W O Q G Q T T M N H H Q
M E P Y V K P      Y C S A C X G
P Y Y R X H M      Y S R P T S G
J W A V C          O O V N D
U K T Y                Y K M L
V A                        H B
```

p26 Q: *Which of these chimps is making a threat and which is frightened?* A: Chimp with pursed lips is making a threat. Chimp baring its teeth is frightened.

p30 Q: *What other characters from ancient myths can you find in the Earth Hall?* A: Medusa turned people to stone. Atlas supported the pillars of the universe.

p31 Word scramble
A: FOSSIL, CORAL, GEMSTONE, CRYSTAL, MINERAL.

p 33 Earth quiz
A:1b, Tsunami; 2c, by lava cooling under the sea; 3a, large crystals form in the rock; 4c, volcanologist.

p34 Q: *Do you know the name for a feature growing down from the roof of a cave?*
A: Stalactite.

p35 Q: *What helps to wear away mountains?*

	M	I	N	E	R	A	L	S			
		E	A	R	T	H					
		C	O	A	L						
			S	T	A	L	A	G	M	I	T	E
			I	C	E						
	F	O	S	S	I	L	S				
	N	U	M	M	U	L	I	T	E	S	

p37 Useful metals
Silver is made into jewellery
Copper is made into wiring
Iron is made into steel
Lead is made into roofing

p37 Q: *Can you name another type of fossil fuel in the gallery?* A: Coal.

p38 Fossil jigsaw

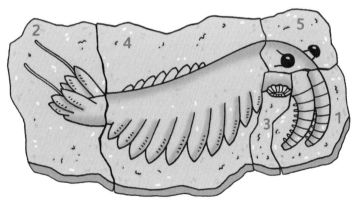

p42 Q: *What is a person who studies meteorites called?* A: Meteoriticist. A meteorologist studies the weather.

p44 Spot the real bits
A: Eyes are made of glass, ears are real, skin is real, teeth are real, tongue is a model.

What is your favourite thing in the Natural History Museum? Draw a picture or stick in a photograph of you and your favourite thing.

This guide is a collaboration between Publishing and the Department for Learning at the Natural History Museum.

© The Trustees of the Natural History Museum, London 2008.
All Rights Reserved.
Reprinted with updates 2014.
ISBN 978 0 565 09238 2

4 6 8 10 9 7 5 3

The Author has asserted her right to be identified as the Author of this work under the Copyright, Designs and Patents Act 1988.

Author: Dr Miranda MacQuitty
Based on some original concepts developed by
Nick Ives and Margarita Petri
Designer: Louise Millar
Illustrator: Jo Moore
Reproduction: Saxon Digital Services
Printer: 10/10 China

Photo credits: © **Andrew R. Milner** p.6 top. © **Anness Publishing/NHMPL** p.20 top, middle. © **Daniel Heuclin/ NHPA** p.11 (Jerboa). © **Geological Society/NHMPL** p.21 bottom left. © **Getty Images** p.11 (grassland, mountains, lion, sahara), p.28 top middle. © **Istockphoto** pp. 3, 8, 10, 11 (sloth, snow leopard, rainforest, swamp, capybara), 12, 14 bottom right, p16 bottom middle, p.25 (sun, hawk), p.26 top left, p.27 bottom right, p.28 bottom right, p.32 middle left, p.34 middle left, p.35 top right, p. 36 bottom right, p.37 bottom middle, right, p.38 top right, p.42 middle, p.43 bottom middle. © **Janos Jurka/NHMPL** p.18 bottom left. © **Jo Moore Illustrations**: pp. 4, 8, 9, 17, 19, p.23 middle right, p.29 middle right, p.30, 33 top left, p.38 bottom, p.39 middle right. © **John Sibbick/NHMPL** p.6 bottom right. © **Matt Stuart** p.8 bottom right. © **Matt Wedel and Mike Taylor** p.5 top. © **Tony Waltham Geophotos** p.34 bottom middle. © **Zephyr/ Science Photo Library** p.32 top. All other images © **The Natural History Museum, London**.

Every effort has been made to contact all copyright holders. If we have been unsuccessful we apologise and welcome correction for future editions and reprints.

Keep in touch

Join our membership for kids
Visit the website www.nhm.ac.uk/kids-only
Natural History Museum, Cromwell Road, London SW7 5BD
T +44 (0)207 942 5000
Opening times:
Monday-Sunday 10.00-17.50
Entrance is free!